W GRATITUDE?

MW01532958

Gratitude is the expression of appreciation for what one has. Practicing gratitude means making conscious efforts to count one's blessings and notice the goodness in life. Try thinking about what or who has made you feel happy.

BEING GRATEFUL...

- keeps you calm and joyful
- boosts mood and self-esteem
- reduces feelings of loneliness and isolation
- helps develop stronger relationships
- improves quality of sleep
- encourages positivity and optimism
- makes life more enjoyable

HOW TO USE THIS JOURNAL:

Each day, try to complete one page. Use colored pencils, gel pens, stickers, photos and anything you would like to personalize this book. Never worry about spelling or grammar. Have fun!

START EACH DAY WITH A GRATEFUL HEART.

A thankful heart is a happy heart.

Affirmations

The power of positive thoughts...
Whenever you can, pick a positive thought to be your theme of the day and repeat it to yourself or write it down and take it with you.

- I am beautiful inside and out.
- I am unique and special.
- I am capable of amazing things.
- I am strong and brave.
- I am kind.
- I am important just because I am me.
- I am doing the best that I can.
- I am good and I am enough.
- I can do hard things.
- I am smart.
- I am loved.
- I am confident ...I believe in myself.
- I can be whoever I want to be.
- I can choose to see the good around me.
- I am not perfect and that's okay.
- I am happy with who I am.

Day 1

Date:

S M T W TH F S ___ / ___ / ___

I'm Thankful for:

1 _____

2 _____

3 _____

I FEEL...

 WHO MADE ME SMILE TODAY...

_____

_____

_____

♡ THE BEST PART OF MY DAY WAS...

DRAW OR WRITE

GRATITUDE ACTIVITY...

Name a person you are grateful for. Think about why you are thankful for this person and how this person made you feel.

What emotions came up in your body and mind during this activity? What action can you take to express your gratitude and appreciation?

Date:

S M T W TH F S ___ / ___ / ___

I'm Thankful for:

1. _____
2. _____
3. _____

I FEEL... 😊 🙂 😐 ☹️

WHO MADE ME SMILE TODAY...

_____
_____
_____

THE BEST PART OF MY DAY WAS...

DRAW OR WRITE

YOU GROW GIRL

Believe you can and you are halfway there...

Think Positive

Five positive thoughts about YOU:

Write one thought in each flower. Then, get out your sparkly pens and crayons to color this bouquet of Positivity.

Are you having trouble thinking of Positive thoughts? Use these questions to help:

What am I good at?

What makes me kind?

What makes me strong?

How do I show love?

How am I a good friend?

How am I unique?

What do I like about me?

Date:

S M T W TH F S   ___ / ___ / ___

>> I'm Thankful for: <<

1 _____

2 _____

3 _____

I FEEL...   😊   🙂   😐   🙁

WHO MADE ME SMILE TODAY...

_____

_____

_____

THE BEST PART OF MY DAY WAS...

DRAW OR WRITE

 # ALL ABOUT ME

Think...then, write or draw

My family:

My friends:

My strengths:

My struggles:

Date:

S M T W TH F S ___ / ___ / ___

I'm Thankful for:

I FEEL...

WHO MADE ME SMILE TODAY...

THE BEST PART OF MY DAY WAS...

DRAW OR WRITE

GRATEFUL FOR MY FRIENDS

What are the names of
your friends?

Draw a friend you are
grateful for.

What are you grateful for
about your friends?

BFF

FRIENDS

I am a good friend.

Date:

S M T W TH F S   ___ / ___ / ___

I'm Thankful for:

1. _____
2. _____
3. _____

I FEEL... 😊 🙂 😐 ☹️

WHO MADE ME SMILE TODAY...

_____

_____

_____

THE BEST PART OF MY DAY WAS...

DRAW OR WRITE

I love ME!

Write words in the petals to describe
yourself and why you are so awesome!

GIRL
POWER

There is only 1 you in this world. You are
special, unique and ONE of a Kind!

Date:

S M T W TH F S ___ / ___ / ___

I'm Thankful for:

1. _____
2. _____
3. _____

I FEEL... 😊 🙂 😐 ☹️

WHO MADE ME SMILE TODAY...

_____
_____
_____

THE BEST PART OF MY DAY WAS...

DRAW OR WRITE

Write a thank you note...

What is the kindest thing someone has done for you lately?

Think about something nice someone has done for you. Write a cute thank you note to tell them how it made you feel.

TODAY IS A GOOD DAY

Date:
_____

People you're thankful for

What is your positive word of the day?

Color in your current mood:

happy   confused   sad

scared   tired   upset

What are you looking forward to tomorrow?

Grateful Doodles

Draw , sketch, and doodle what you are thankful for.. Make a collage..

Date:

S M T W TH F S ___ / ___ / ___

I'm Thankful for:

1

2

3

I FEEL...

WHO MADE ME SMILE TODAY...

♡ THE BEST PART OF MY DAY WAS...

DRAW OR WRITE

THE BEST WAY TO BE HAPPY IS TO BE KIND

IN A SMALL WAY YOU ARE CHANGING THE WORLD

How did someone show kindness today?

_____

_____

_____

Sometimes the best way to show kindness is
simply to give a smile.

Date:

S M T W TH F S ___ / ___ / ___

I'm Thankful for:

1. _____
2. _____
3. _____

I FEEL...

WHO MADE ME SMILE TODAY...

_____
_____
_____

THE BEST PART OF MY DAY WAS...

DRAW OR WRITE

AFFIRMATIONS

Brainstorm words to positively describe yourself. Use crayons or sparkly pens and write them in the jar.

Date:

S M T W TH F S ___ / ___ / ___

I'm Thankful for:

1. _____

2. _____

3. _____

I FEEL... 😊 🙂 😐 ☹️

WHO MADE ME SMILE TODAY...

_____

_____

_____

THE BEST PART OF MY DAY WAS...

DRAW OR WRITE

MY GRATITUDE HAND

Each day, use the fingers of your hand to think of five people, places, or things you are grateful for in your life. Use this page to write down all the things you are grateful for today. You can do this anytime or place.

1. _____
2. _____
3. _____
4. _____
5. _____

Think POSITIVE

Showing gratitude is like giving a little gift every time you share it.

TODAY IS A GOOD DAY

Date:
_____

People you're thankful for

What is your positive word of the day?

Color in your current mood:

happy   confused   sad

scared   tired   upset

What are you looking forward to tomorrow?
_____

Activity: DRAW OR WRITE ABOUT A PEACEFUL PLACE OR MOMENT THAT MAKES YOU FEEL AT EASE. 🙂

THIS IS MY HAPPY PLACE

"Most folks are as happy as they make up their minds to be."
- Abraham Lincoln

Date:

S M T W TH F S ___ / ___ / ___

I'm Thankful for:

1
2
3

I FEEL...

WHO MADE ME SMILE TODAY...

THE BEST PART OF MY DAY WAS...

DRAW OR WRITE

6 THINGS THAT MAKE MY HEART SMILE ♡‿♡

Fill each heart with something that makes you happy.

Happiness is a daily choice. Think about what makes you the happiest. ♥

Date:

S M T W TH F S _____ / _____ / _____

I'm Thankful for:

1 _____

2 _____

3 _____

I FEEL... 😊 🙂 😐 🙁

WHO MADE ME SMILE TODAY...

_____

_____

_____

THE BEST PART OF MY DAY WAS...

DRAW OR WRITE

Be happy not because everything is good, but because you can see the good side of everything.

Daily Affirmation

As you color, think of a positive thought for the day:

My positive thought is...

_____

_____

_____

_____

Date:
S M T W TH F S ___ / ___ / ___

I'm Thankful for:

1. _____
2. _____
3. _____

I FEEL...   😊 🙂 😐 🙁

⭐ WHO MADE ME SMILE TODAY...
_____
_____
_____

☆ THE BEST PART OF MY DAY WAS...

DRAW OR WRITE

I AM STROKE

I AM STRONG

I can do hard things... I just have to put my mind to it!

What is something
you are proud of?

As you color, think of a positive thought for the day ...

_____

_____

_____

_____

TODAY IS A GOOD DAY

Date:

_____

People you're thankful for

What is your positive word of the day?

Color in your current mood:

happy

confused

sad

scared

tired

upset

What are you looking forward to tomorrow?

YOU BECOME WHAT YOU BELIEVE

As you color, think of a way to be more positive
about something in your life.
This is practicing looking at the bright side and
sometimes it's hard to do.

Date:

S M T W TH F S ___ / ___ / ___

I'm Thankful for:

1. _____

2. _____

3. _____

I FEEL... 😊 🙂 😐 ☹️

WHO MADE ME SMILE TODAY...

_____
_____
_____

♡ THE BEST PART OF MY DAY WAS...

DRAW OR WRITE

Today I am most thankful for...

_____

_____

_____

BEE THANKFUL

Thought of the Day...

Gratitude is a daily choice. Each day we decide to be happy, positive and thankful.

Date:

S M T W TH F S ___/___/___

I'm Thankful for:

1. _____
2. _____
3. _____

I FEEL... 😊 🙂 😐 ☹️

WHO MADE ME SMILE TODAY...

_____
_____
_____

THE BEST PART OF MY DAY WAS...

DRAW OR WRITE

It's cool to be kind.

There are so many ways to show kindness...

As you color, think about Kindness...

Who shows you kindness and How does it make you feel?

_____

_____

_____

_____

_____

Date:

S M T W TH F S ___ / ___ / ___

I'm Thankful for:

1. _____

2. _____

3. _____

I FEEL... 😊 🙂 😐 🙁

WHO MADE ME SMILE TODAY...

_____

_____

_____

THE BEST PART OF MY DAY WAS...

DRAW OR WRITE

Let's TACO 'bout friendship!

I am thankful for my friends.

Decorate this taco with words, stickers or pictures about what makes you thankful for your friends and pets.

A true friend is someone who makes it easy to be yourself.

Date:

S M T W TH F S ___ / ___ / ___

I'm Thankful for:

1. _____
2. _____
3. _____

I FEEL... 😊 🙂 😐 ☹️

WHO MADE ME SMILE TODAY...

_____
_____
_____

♡ THE BEST PART OF MY DAY WAS...

DRAW OR WRITE

Ha Ha Ha
Ha Ha
... Ha Ha

Happy ☺

Fill this heart with Happy Thoughts..
what made you laugh? Can you think of something
really _funny_?..

Date:

S M T W TH F S ___/___/___

I'm Thankful for:

1 _____

2 _____

3 _____

I FEEL...

WHO MADE ME SMILE TODAY...

_____

_____

_____

THE BEST PART OF MY DAY WAS...

DRAW OR WRITE

ALL about ME!

by...................

My favourite colour is...

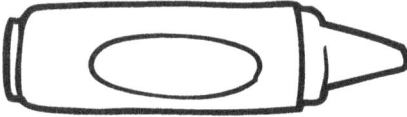

I am thankful for ME...

This is me!

My favourite food is...

I'm .... years old.

My favourite animal is...

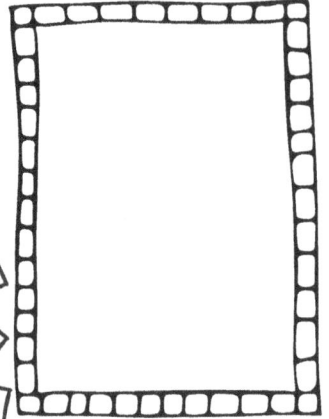

My favourite TV show is...

Date:

S M T W TH F S ___/___/___

I'm Thankful for:

1. _____

2. _____

3. _____

I FEEL... 😊 🙂 😐 ☹️

WHO MADE ME SMILE TODAY...

_____

_____

_____

THE BEST PART OF MY DAY WAS...

DRAW OR WRITE

TODAY IS A GOOD DAY

Date: _____

People you're thankful for

What is your positive word of the day?

[   ]

Color in your current mood:

happy   confused   sad

scared   tired   upset

What are you looking forward to tomorrow?

MY DREAMS

In the cloud, draw your hopes and dreams for the future. What do you wish would happen...

Tonight before you fall asleep, think of a thankful thought...

HAPPY HEARTS

Choosing to be happy is easier when you practice it everyday!

Today I am happy about...

_____

_____

Date:

S M T W TH F S ___ / ___ / ___

I'm Thankful for:

1. _____
2. _____
3. _____

I FEEL...

WHO MADE ME SMILE TODAY...

_____
_____
_____

THE BEST PART OF MY DAY WAS...

DRAW OR WRITE

TINY GALLERY OF POSITIVITY

Draw yourself with people and things that make you happy.

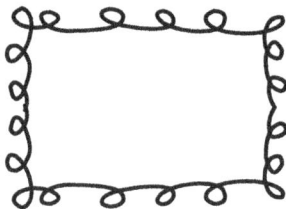

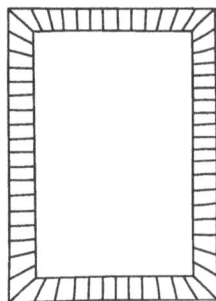

Date:

S M T W TH F S ___ / ___ / ___

I'm Thankful for:

1. _____
2. _____
3. _____

I FEEL... 😊 🙂 😐 ☹️

WHO MADE ME SMILE TODAY...

_____
_____
_____

THE BEST PART OF MY DAY WAS...

DRAW OR WRITE

COLOR AND THINK OF THINGS THAT MAKE YOUR HEART HAPPY.

TODAY I AM HAPPY ABOUT...

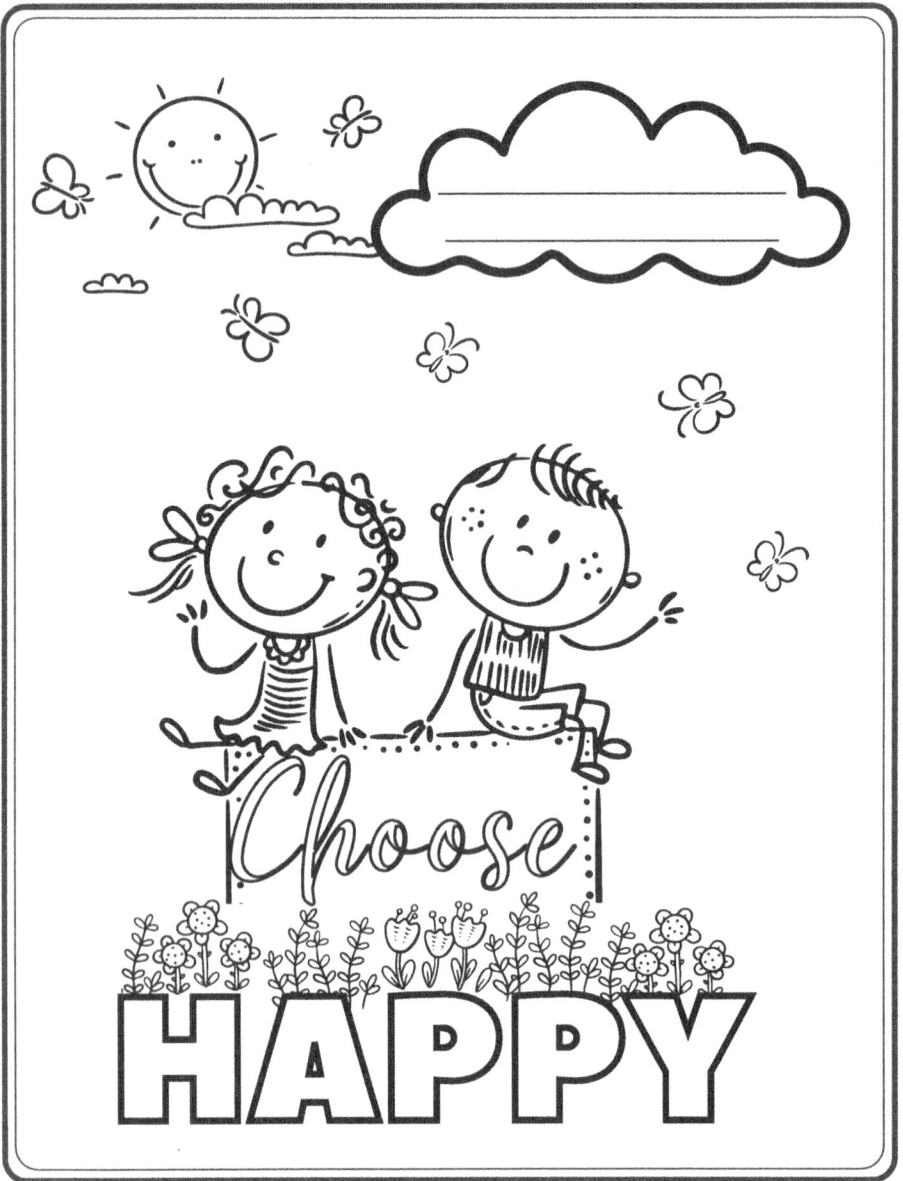

Be happy for all the little things... over time they add up!

Date:
S M T W TH F S __ / __ / __

I'm Thankful for:

 _____

 _____

 _____

I FEEL...

 **WHO MADE ME SMILE TODAY...**

_____

_____

_____

THE BEST PART OF MY DAY WAS...

DRAW OR WRITE

THINK Positive

AS YOU COLOR, THINK OF AS MANY
HAPPY & POSITIVE THOUGHTS AS YOU CAN
HOW MANY CAN YOU THINK OF?

TODAY IS A GOOD DAY

Date:
_____

People you're thankful for

What is your positive word of the day?

Color in your current mood:

happy   confused   sad

scared   tired   upset

What are you looking forward to tomorrow?

THIS IS ME

Draw or glue picture

THINGS I LIKE... 🙂

THINGS I DISLIKE... 🙁

MY FAVORITE THING ABOUT ME..

Date:

S M T W TH F S ___ / ___ / ___

I'm Thankful for:

1 _____

2 _____

3 _____

I FEEL... 😊 🙂 😐 ☹️

WHO MADE ME SMILE TODAY...

_____
_____
_____

♡ THE BEST PART OF MY DAY WAS...

DRAW OR WRITE

I AM THINKING
POSITIVE

MY POSITIVE
THOUGHT OF THE DAY IS

PRACTICING GRATITUDE
MAKES YOUR HEART HAPPY

Date:

S M T W TH F S ___ / ___ / ___

I'm Thankful for:

1 _____
2 _____
3 _____

I FEEL... 😊 🙂 😐 ☹️

WHO MADE ME SMILE TODAY...
_____
_____
_____

THE BEST PART OF MY DAY WAS...

DRAW OR WRITE

5 THINGS

THAT MAKE ME HAPPY TODAY

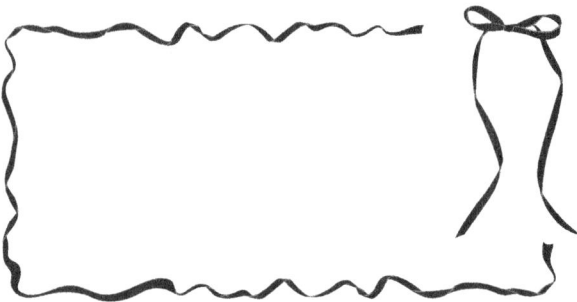

Date:

S M T W TH F S ___ / ___ / ___

I'm Thankful for:

I FEEL...

WHO MADE ME SMILE TODAY...

_____
_____
_____

THE BEST PART OF MY DAY WAS...

DRAW OR WRITE

GRATEFUL FOR NATURE

Draw your favorite
place in nature.

What is your favorite
activity to do outdoors?

Which season are you most
grateful for?

What animal are you most
grateful for?

BE THE SUNSHINE

TODAY IS A GOOD DAY

Date:
_____

People you're thankful for

What is your positive word of the day?

Color in your current mood:

happy

confused

sad

scared

tired

upset

What are you looking forward to tomorrow?

Gratitude changes Everything

AS YOU COLOR, THINK ABOUT WHAT YOU
ARE MOST GRATEFUL FOR TODAY

Date:

S M T W TH F S ___ / ___ / ___

I'm Thankful for:

1.

2.

3.

I FEEL...

😊 🙂 😐 🙁

♡ WHO MADE ME SMILE TODAY...

♡ THE BEST PART OF MY DAY WAS...

DRAW OR WRITE

LOVE

Fill this heart with people and things
you love...

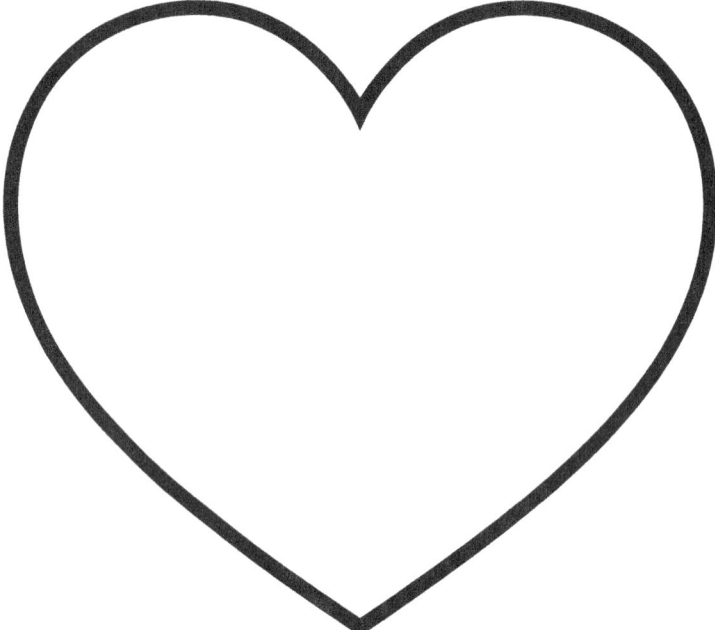

When you are thankful for what you have,
it seems like more than enough.

LOVE

Date:

S M T W TH F S ___ / ___ / ___

I'm Thankful for:

1. _____
2. _____
3. _____

I FEEL... 😊 🙂 😐 🙁

WHO MADE ME SMILE TODAY...

_____
_____
_____

THE BEST PART OF MY DAY WAS...

DRAW OR WRITE

Sprinkle Kindness

My favorite way to show kindness is...

_____

_____

_____

_____

_____

Date:

S M T W TH F S ___/___/___

I'm Thankful for:

1. _____

2. _____

3. _____

I FEEL... 😊 🙂 😐 🙁

☆ WHO MADE ME SMILE TODAY...

_____

_____

_____

☆ THE BEST PART OF MY DAY WAS...

DRAW OR WRITE

DRAW
THREE THINGS
that you are grateful for today

Being kind and grateful never goes out of style!

TODAY IS A GOOD DAY

Date:
_____

People you're thankful for

What is your positive word of the day?

Color in your current mood:

happy

confused

sad

scared

tired

upset

What are you looking forward to tomorrow?
_____

Today
I am Thankful for...

_____

_____

_____

_____

THANKFUL THOUGHT:
WRITE A CUTE THANK YOU NOTE TO SOMEONE WHO HAS DONE SOMETHING NICE FOR YOU. IT COULD BE FOR A FAMILY MEMBER, FRIEND OR TEACHER.

Date:

S M T W TH F S ___/___/___

I'm Thankful for:

1. _____

2. _____

3. _____

I FEEL... 😊 🙂 😐 ☹️

WHO MADE ME SMILE TODAY...

_____

_____

_____

♡ THE BEST PART OF MY DAY WAS...

DRAW OR WRITE

GRATITUDE

TODAY I AM THANKFUL FOR...

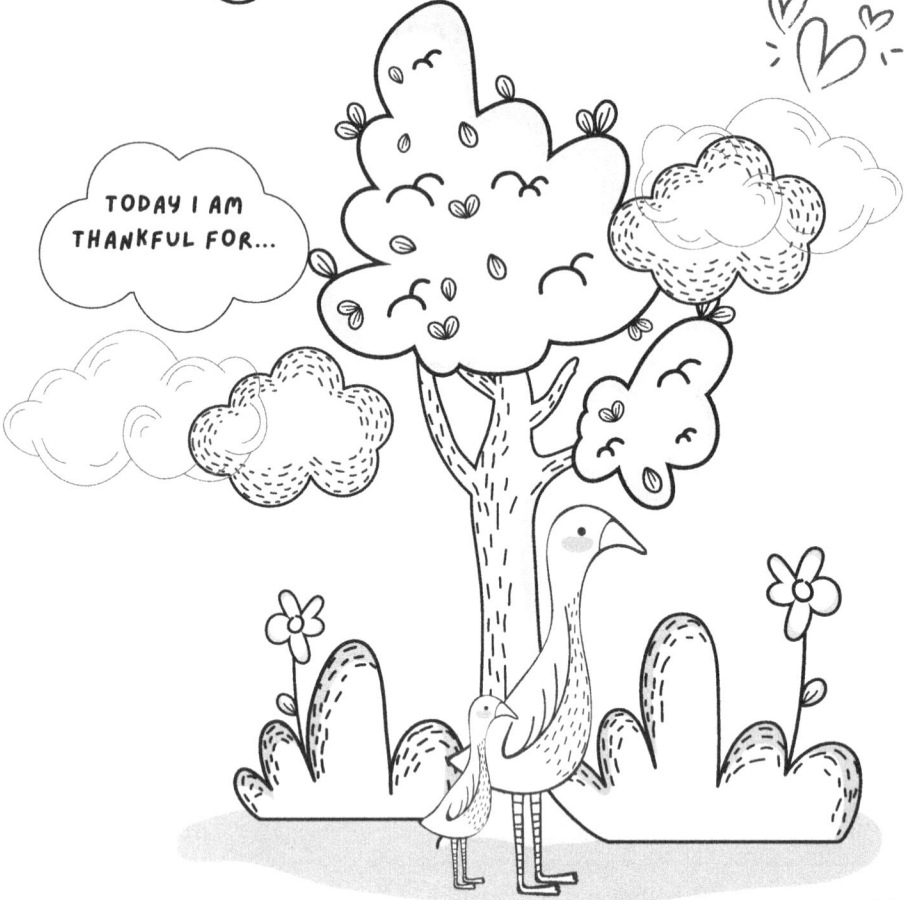

ATTITUDE

1 _____

2 _____

3 _____

As you color, think about your day and make a list of three thankful or positive thoughts of the day.

Date:

S M T W TH F S ___/___/___

I'm Thankful for:

1. _____
2. _____
3. _____

I FEEL... 😊 🙂 😐 🙁

WHO MADE ME SMILE TODAY...

_____
_____
_____

THE BEST PART OF MY DAY WAS...

DRAW OR WRITE

Positive Vibes

What you choose to focus on will grow...

Change your thinking and you will change your feelings...

happy

strong

love

grateful

joy

confidant

kind

friendhip

Daily Affirmation

As you color, think of a positive thought for the day ...

_____

_____

_____

Date:
S M T W TH F S ___ / ___ / ___

I'm Thankful for:

 _____

 _____

 _____

I FEEL...

 WHO MADE ME SMILE TODAY...

_____

_____

_____

THE BEST PART OF MY DAY WAS...

DRAW OR WRITE

When it Rains look for Rainbows

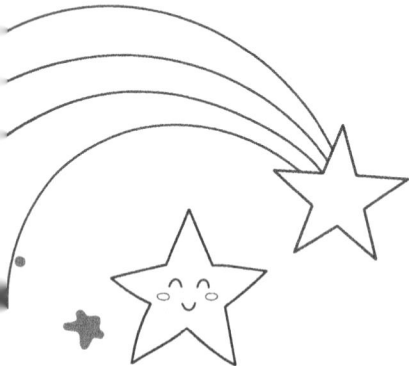

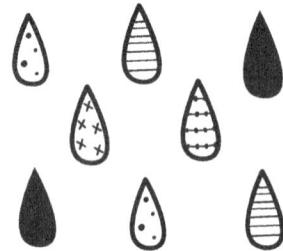

When its Dark look for Stars

As you color, think of a way to be more positive about something in your life.

TODAY IS A GOOD DAY

Date:
_____

People you're thankful for

What is your positive word of the day?

Color in your current mood:

happy   confused   sad

scared   tired   upset

What are you looking forward to tomorrow?
_____

THE THINGS I LOVE

My favorite activity

My favorite movie, show or book

My favorite school subject

Favorite color

Thankful for
everything I love

Favorite food

Favorite place

Date:

S M T W TH F S ___ / ___ / ___

I'm Thankful for:

1. _____

2. _____

3. _____

I FEEL... 😊 🙂 😐 🙁

♡ WHO MADE ME SMILE TODAY...

_____

_____

_____

♡ THE BEST PART OF MY DAY WAS...

DRAW OR WRITE

Color and think of 2 happy thoughts...

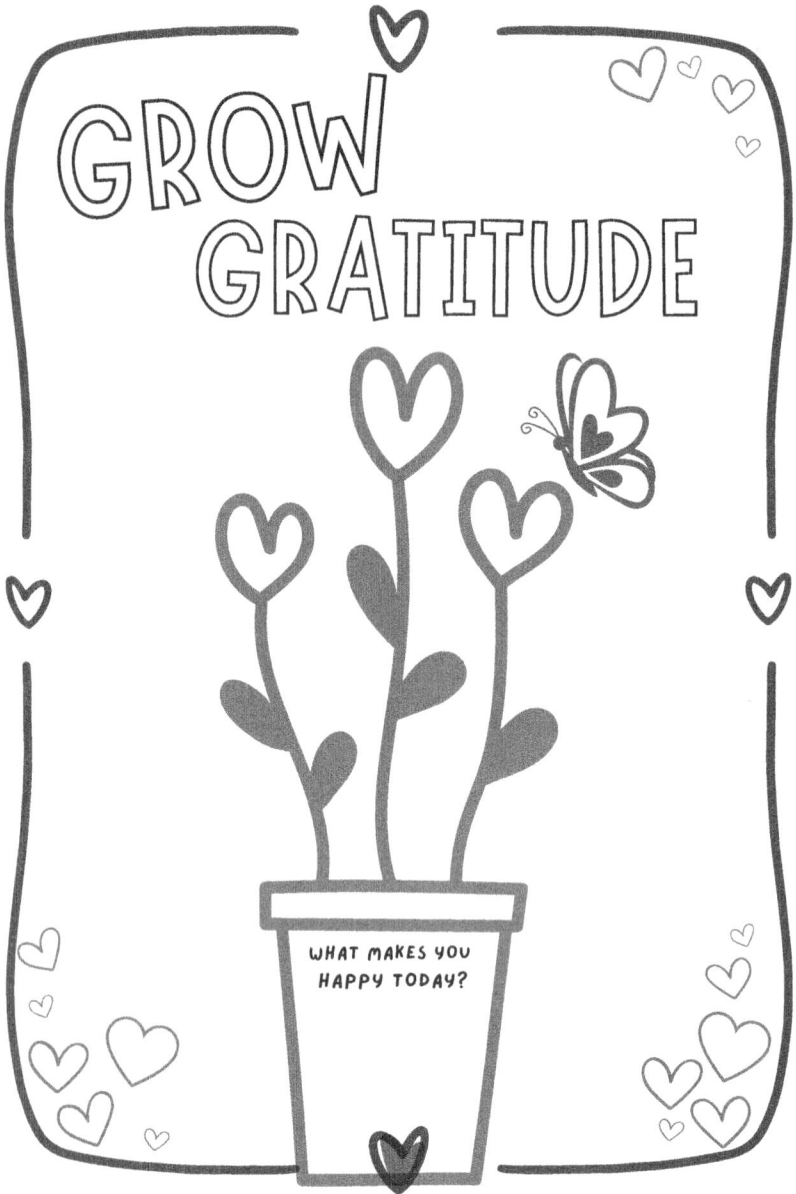

GROW GRATITUDE

WHAT MAKES YOU
HAPPY TODAY?

1. _____

2. _____

Date:

S M T W TH F S ___/___/___

I'm Thankful for:

1 _____

2 _____

3 _____

I FEEL...

WHO MADE ME SMILE TODAY...

_____

_____

_____

THE BEST PART OF MY DAY WAS...

DRAW OR WRITE

POSITIVE
THOUGHT OF THE DAY

Don't be so hard on yourself...your still growing.

Affirmation:
I am amazing.
I can do hard things.

Today was a good day because... _____

_____

Date:

S M T W TH F S ___/___/___

I'm Thankful for:

1 _____

2 _____

3 _____

I FEEL... 😊 🙂 😐 🙁

WHO MADE ME SMILE TODAY...

_____

_____

_____

THE BEST PART OF MY DAY WAS...

DRAW OR WRITE

Happy Day Memories

What was a special day that you are thankful for?
Draw or glue pictures to remember how you felt that day ...

Date:

S M T W TH F S ___ / ___ / ___

I'm Thankful for:

1. _____
2. _____
3. _____

I FEEL... 😊 🙂 😐 ☹️

WHO MADE ME SMILE TODAY...

_____
_____
_____

♡ THE BEST PART OF MY DAY WAS...

DRAW OR WRITE

I AM HAPPY

Happiness is beauty that
shines from the inside out.

1. _____

2. _____

COLOR AND THINK OF TWO HAPPY THOUGHTS

Date:

S M T W TH F S ___/___/___

I'm Thankful for:

1. _____
2. _____
3. _____

I FEEL... 😊 🙂 😐 ☹️

WHO MADE ME SMILE TODAY...

_____
_____
_____

THE BEST PART OF MY DAY WAS...

DRAW OR WRITE

Today
IS A GOOD DAY
TO LOOK ON THE BRIGHT SIDE

As you color, think about what it means to look on the bright side. Sometimes it isn't easy to see the good side of a situation.

WHAT WERE THE 3 BEST PARTS OF TODAY...

1 _____

2 _____

3 _____

Date:

S M T W TH F S ___ / ___ / ___

I'm Thankful for:

1
2
3

I FEEL... 😊 🙂 😐 🙁

♡ WHO MADE ME SMILE TODAY...

♡ THE BEST PART OF MY DAY WAS...

DRAW OR WRITE

THE BEST PART OF TODAY...

Draw or Write

Think about your day...

Did something make you laugh?
What is something you are
thankful for today?

When we are focused on being thankful and looking for the good of the day we can't be unhappy at the same time.

Date:

S M T W TH F S ___/___/___

I'm Thankful for:

1. _____
2. _____
3. _____

I FEEL... 😊 🙂 😐 ☹️

WHO MADE ME SMILE TODAY...

_____
_____
_____

THE BEST PART OF MY DAY WAS...

DRAW OR WRITE

GRATITUDE
ATTITUDE

Gratitude grows over time through our daily actions. Each small choice we make, to see the good in situations or to appreciate the people around us, helps us develop a grateful heart.

As you color, think about what you are most thankful for today

TODAY I AM MOST GRATEFUL FOR:

_____

_____

Date:

S M T W TH F S ___ / ___ / ___

I'm Thankful for:

1. _____
2. _____
3. _____

I FEEL... 😊 🙂 😐 ☹️

WHO MADE ME SMILE TODAY...

_____
_____
_____

THE BEST PART OF MY DAY WAS...

DRAW OR WRITE

DATE:_____

GRATITUDE REFLECTION

WRITE AND DRAW WHAT YOU ARE GRATEFUL
FOR TODAY:

_____

_____

_____

DESCRIBE WHAT YOU LOVE ABOUT YOURSELF:

_____

_____

_____

DESCRIBE WHAT YOU ARE EXCITED ABOUT:

_____

_____

_____

TODAY IS A GOOD DAY

Date:
_____

People you're thankful for

What is your positive word of the day?

Color in your current mood:

happy

confused

sad

scared

tired

upset

What are you looking forward to tomorrow?
_____

MY GRATITUDE ATTITUDE

I can do hard things.

SOMETHING I LEARNED

SOMETHING I'M PROUD OF

TODAY'S AFFIRMATION ~POSITIVE THOUGHT

TOMORROW I LOOK FORWARD TO

NOTES

Date:

S M T W TH F S ___/___/___

I'm Thankful for:

1 _____

2 _____

3 _____

I FEEL... 😊 🙂 😐 ☹️

♥ WHO MADE ME SMILE TODAY...

_____

_____

_____

♡ THE BEST PART OF MY DAY WAS...

DRAW OR WRITE

GRATITUDE

AS YOU COLOR, THINK ABOUT WHERE YOU LIVE ...

WHAT IS YOUR FAVOIRTE THING ABOUT YOUR NEIGHBORHOOD?

_____

_____

_____

_____

_____

Date:

S M T W TH F S ___ / ___ / ___

I'm Thankful for:

1. _____
2. _____
3. _____

I FEEL... 😊 🙂 😐 ☹️

WHO MADE ME SMILE TODAY...

_____
_____
_____

THE BEST PART OF MY DAY WAS...

DRAW OR WRITE

THE THINGS I LOVE

L♡VE YOURSELF

LOVE YOURSELF unconditionally. There is only one you, and that is what makes you special.
♡♡♡♡♡

What I love about my family

What I love about my school

I love this color

I love this smell

I love this weather

 I ♥ Me

Date:

S M T W TH F S ___ / ___ / ___

I'm Thankful for:

1. _____

2. _____

3. _____

I FEEL... 😊 🙂 😐 🙁

WHO MADE ME SMILE TODAY...

_____

_____

_____

THE BEST PART OF MY DAY WAS...

DRAW OR WRITE

ME

Today I am happy about...

Today I feel most thankful for:

Positive word of the day.

I learned that...

I love me because

Decorate this page as you fill it in.

Thank you

If you enjoyed this book, please consider leaving a quick review on Amazon. Positive reviews from wonderful customers help other parents feel confident about choosing this book. Sharing your happy experience will be greatly appreciated.

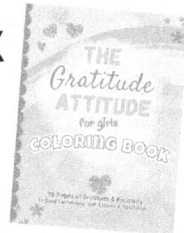

Made in the USA
Monee, IL
16 June 2025